Help the
Orangutans

by Grace Hansen

LITTLE ACTIVISTS:
ENDANGERED SPECIES

Abdo Kids Jumbo is an Imprint of Abdo Kids
abdobooks.com

abdobooks.com

Published by Abdo Kids, a division of ABDO, P.O. Box 398166, Minneapolis, Minnesota 55439.
Copyright © 2019 by Abdo Consulting Group, Inc. International copyrights reserved in all countries.
No part of this book may be reproduced in any form without written permission from the publisher.
Abdo Kids Jumbo™ is a trademark and logo of Abdo Kids.

102018

012019

 THIS BOOK CONTAINS RECYCLED MATERIALS

Photo Credits: iStock, Shutterstock

Production Contributors: Teddy Borth, Jennie Forsberg, Grace Hansen

Design Contributors: Dorothy Toth, Laura Mitchell

Library of Congress Control Number: 2018946054
Publisher's Cataloging-in-Publication Data

Names: Hansen, Grace, author.
Title: Help the orangutans / by Grace Hansen.
Description: Minneapolis, Minnesota : Abdo Kids, 2019 | Series: Little activists:
    endangered species | Includes glossary, index and online resources (page 24).
Identifiers: ISBN 9781532182020 (lib. bdg.) | ISBN 9781532183003 (ebook) |
    ISBN 9781532183492 (Read-to-me ebook)
Subjects: LCSH: Orangutans--Juvenile literature. | Wildlife recovery--Juvenile
    literature. | Endangered species--Juvenile literature. | Deforestation--Tropics--
    Juvenile literature.
Classification: DDC 333.954--dc23

Table of Contents

Orangutans

Orangutans are found on only two Asian islands. They live in the rain forests of Borneo and Sumatra.

Borneo

Sumatra

5

Orangutans spend most

of their lives in trees.

They even sleep in trees.

They build nests up in branches.
They cover themselves with
large leaves. This protects them
from the rains.

9

Status

Orangutans are considered **endangered**. They face many threats.

10

The greatest threat is habitat loss. Fewer trees means less food and safe places for the apes.

13

Illegal hunting and **trade** is also an issue. Baby orangutans are taken from their mothers. They are sold as pets.

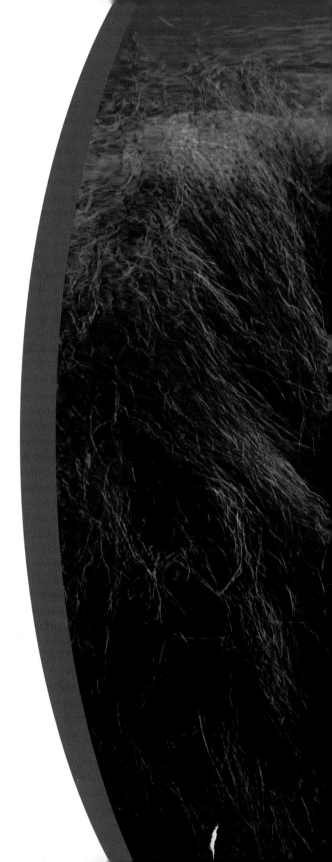

Female orangutans give birth just once every 5 to 10 years. This makes it harder to get population numbers back up.

Why They Matter

Orangutans are very smart.
They are close relatives of
humans. We share 97% of
our **DNA** with them.

Orangutans move throughout their habitat. They eat lots of plants. This scatters seeds, helping more plants grow.

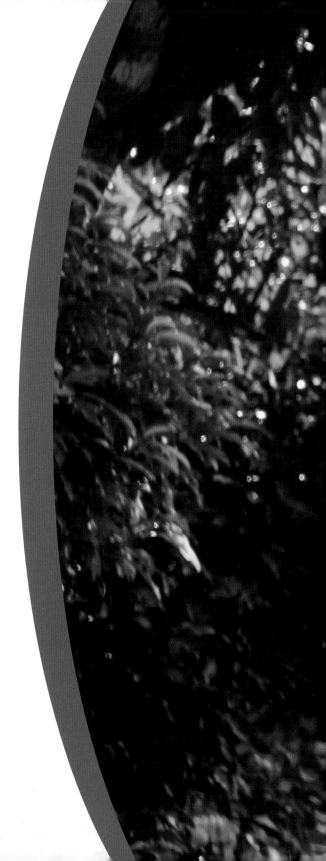

Orangutans Overview

- Status: **Endangered** (Bornean) and Critically Endangered (Sumatran)

- Population: 104,700 Bornean and 7,500 Sumatran orangutans

- Habitat: Tropical rain forests of Borneo and Sumatra

- Greatest Threats: Habitat loss and illegal hunting and **trade**

Glossary

DNA – an abbreviation for deoxyribonucleic acid, a substance found in cells that contains information about the characteristics of a living thing.

endangered – in danger of becoming extinct.

trade – the act of selling.

23

Index

Abdo Kids ONLINE
FREE! ONLINE MULTIMEDIA RESOURCES

Visit **abdokids.com** and use this code to access crafts, games, videos, and more!

Abdo Kids Code:
LHK2020